The Mischief Makers

A Series of Shenanigans and Brotherly Love

Written by: Christie Cuthbert

Illustrated by: Waleed Ahmad

Cuthbert 2021 ♡

To John, Tommy, Teddy, Nate and Brewster, the real *Mischief Makers*, thank you for always making me laugh.

I am so lucky to be your Mom. xoxo

Eddie, Teddy, and Freddy Banks, were masters of mischief, princes of pranks.

Big brother, Simon, and little dog, Stew, were always annoyed at things they would do.

1

Sneaking sweets in church (yum!), making green bean milkshakes, these triplets were a menace for goodness sakes!

2

Dancing on the table, hiding Dad's keys, tricking Simon with pepper, making him sneeze.

"Go up to your room!" their Mom would roar!

They'd snicker (hee hee!) knowing more fun was in store.

One afternoon on a boring old day,
the Banks boys shot spit wads (fling!) as they started to play.

"Let's invent something great!" Freddy said with a grin.
"A bone launcher for Stew! That's for sure a win!"

They gathered parts from all over their home,
pipe cleaners, boxes, soda cans and foam.

Trinkets and treasures were thrown in a pile
(clink!), silverware Mom won't see for a while.

Chewing gum, hangers and a paper plate,
old trophies – how perfect for what they'd create!

Hours later their invention was done,
it was time to test it and have some fun!

The boys were excited and told Stew to get ready,
but big trouble was brewing for Eddie,

Freddy,

and Teddy.

See, the dog bone biscuit in their creative plan,
instead of shooting outward, flew up into
the fan (whoops!)

It bounced off the TV, a lamp and a mirror, broke through the window, filling the boys with fear (oh no!).

"We'll tell Mom it was a Zombie, giving us a fright!"

"Or maybe a racoon did it, looking for a bite."

12

"We can hide in our beds, pretending we're napping."

"We'll tell her it shattered while a bird was tapping."

WOOF

As the triplets fought over what lies to tell,
big brother Simon knew the right answer well.

"It's one heck of a mess and Mom will be mad, but if you tell the truth, in time you'll be glad.

You'll be in more trouble if you tell a lie, honesty is the best policy and here's why.

To be a good person, someone to trust, owning your actions in life is a must.

Right now you three have a big choice to make, to tell the real story or something fake.

Simon was right, (sigh) and they gathered their strength, confessing their entire story at length.

You're Doomed...

Their Mom lost her marbles and swept up the glass,
but was proud of their honesty and let it pass.

"Accidents happen and this one is a mess, but I'm proud of you for being honest enough to confess."

"Encouraging each other to do what's right, will make you feel good when you sleep at night."

As they hugged their Mom, the boys glanced at the floor,
and noticed their launcher vanished out the door!

They quickly ran to the yard only to find,
the mischievous Stew launching dog bones just fine.

The End

Made in the USA
Columbia, SC
16 February 2021